My Meaningful Life

Copyright © 2020 Joel Kongaika

All rights reserved.

ISBN: 9798605342557

this record of meaning belongs to

"It's impossible to have a meaningful conversation about happiness without understanding what makes each of us tick. When we find ourselves stuck in unhappy careers—and even unhappy lives—it is often the result of a fundamental misunderstanding of what really motivates us."

— Clayton M. Christensen, *How Will You Measure Your Life?*

An incredibly meaningful life of innovating and inspiring!
Thank you, Mr. Christensen.

Clayton M. Christensen
1952-2020

JOURNALING GUIDANCE

each page starts with

THIS IS WHAT _____________ **MEANS TO ME:**
(to focus your thoughts)

and ends with

THAT IS WHAT _____________ **MEANS TO ME.**
(to exclaim your meaning)

fill in the blanks with important

VALUES

RELATIONSHIPS

PLACES

EVENTS

BELIEFS

MOTIVATIONS

PRACTICES

and all things of meaning to you and yours…

then choose one or more ways to express your reflections

write it

doodle it

paint it

storify it

quote it

list it

humanize it

celebrate it

gamify it

songify it

solve it

study it

graph it

map it

voice it

paraphrase it

discuss it

research it

sleep on it

capture it

expand it

ponder it

create it

embrace it

get started

select any of
these five hundred
examples of values

Abundance
Acceptance
Accessibility
Accomplishment
Accountability
Accuracy
Achievement
Acknowledgement
Activeness
Adaptability
Adoration
Advancement
Adventure
Adventurousness
Affection
Affluence
Aggressiveness
Agility
Alertness
Altruism
Amazement
Ambition
Amusement
Anticipation
Appreciation
Approachability
Approval
Art
Articulacy
Artistry
Assertiveness
Assurance
Attentive
Attentiveness
Attractiveness
Audacity
Authenticity
Authority
Autonomy
Availability
Awareness
Awe
Balance
Beauty
Being the best
Belonging
Benevolence

Bliss
Boldness
Bravery
Brilliance
Buoyancy
Calm
Calmness
Camaraderie
Candor
Capability
Capable
Carefulness
Celebrity
Certainty
Challenge
Change
Charity
Charm
Chastity
Cheerfulness
Citizenship
Clarity
Cleanliness
Clear-mindedness
Clever
Cleverness
Closeness
Comfort
Commitment
Common sense
Communication
Community
Compassion
Competence
Competency
Competition
Competitiveness
Completion
Composure
Concentration
Confidence
Conformity
Congruency
Connection
Consciousness
Conservation
Consistency

Contentment
Continuity
Continuous
Improvement
Contribution
Control
Conviction
Conviviality
Coolness
Cooperation
Cordiality
Correctness
Country
Courage
Courtesy
Craftiness
Creation
Creativity
Credibility
Cunning
Curiosity
Daring
Decisive
Decisiveness
Decorum
Dedication
Deference
Delight
Democraticness
Dependability
Depth
Desire
Determination
Development
Devotion
Devoutness
Dexterity
Dignity
Diligence
Direction
Directness
Discipline
Discovery
Discretion
Diversity
Dominance
Dreaming

Drive
Duty
Dynamism
Eagerness
Ease
Economy
Ecstasy
Education
Effectiveness
Efficiency
Elation
Elegance
Empathy
Empower
Encouragement
Endurance
Energy
Enjoyment
Entertainment
Enthusiasm
Environmentalism
Equality
Ethical
Ethics
Euphoria
Excellence
Excitement
Exhilaration
Expectancy
Expediency
Experience
Expertise
Exploration
Expressive
Expressiveness
Extravagance
Extroversion
Exuberance
Fairness
Faith
Fame
Family
Family-orientedness
Famous
Fascination
Fashion
Fearless

Fearlessness
Feelings
Ferocious
Ferocity
Fidelity
Fierceness
Financial
   independence
Firmness
Fitness
Flexibility
Flow
Fluency
Focus
Foresight
Fortitude
Frankness
Freedom
Friendliness
Friendship
Friendships
Frugality
Fun
Gallantry
Generosity
Genius
Gentility
Giving
Good humor
Goodness
Grace
Gratitude
Greatness
Gregariousness
Growth
Guidance
Happiness
Hard Work
Harmony
Health
Heart
Helpfulness
Helping Society
Heroism
Holiness
Honesty
Honor

Hope
Hopefulness
Hospitality
Humility
Humor
Hygiene
Imagination
Impact
Impartiality
Improvement
Independence
Individuality
Industry
Influence
Ingenuity
Inner Harmony
Innovation
Inquisitive
Inquisitiveness
Insightful
Insightfulness
Inspiration
Inspiring
Integrity
Intellect
Intellectual Status
Intelligence
Intensity
Intimacy
Intrepidness
Introspection
Introversion
Intuition
Intuitive
Intuitiveness
Inventiveness
Investing
Involvement
Irreverent
Joy
Judiciousness
Justice
Keenness
Kindness
Knowledge
Lawful
Leadership

Learning
Legacy
Liberation
Liberty
Lightness
Liveliness
Logic
Longevity
Love
Loyalty
Majesty
Making a difference
Marriage
Mastery
Maturity
Meaning
Meaningful Work
Meekness
Mellowness
Merit
Meticulousness
Mindfulness
Moderation
Modesty
Motivation
Mysteriousness
Nature
Neatness
Nerve
Noncomformity
Obedience
Open-mindedness
Openness
Optimism
Order
Organization
Originality
Outdoors
Outlandishness
Outrageousness
Partnership
Passion
Patience
Patriotism
Peace
Perceptiveness
Perfection

Performance
Perkiness
Perseverance
Persistence
Persuasiveness
Philanthropy
Piety
Playfulness
Pleasantness
Pleasure
Poise
Polish
Popularity
Positivity
Potency
Potential
Power
Practicality
Pragmatism
Precision
Preparedness
Presence
Present
Pride
Privacy
Proactivity
Productivity
Professionalism
Prosperity
Prudence
Punctuality
Purity
Purpose
Quality
Quality-orientation
Rationality
Realism
Realistic
Reason
Reasonableness
Recognition
Recreation
Refinement
Reflection
Reflective
Relaxation
Reliability

Relief
Religion
Religiousness
Reputation
Resilience
Resolution
Resolve
Resourcefulness
Respect
Responsibility
Rest
Restraint
Results-oriented
Reverence
Richness
Rigor
Risk
Sacredness
Sacrifice
Saintliness
Satisfaction
Science
Security
Self-actualization
Self-control
Self-reliance
Self-Respect
Selfless
Selflessness
Sensitivity
Sensuality
Serenity
Service
Service to others
Sexiness
Sexuality
Sharing
Shrewdness
Significance
Silence
Silliness
Simplicity
Sincerity
Skill
Skillfulness
Smart
Solidarity

My Meaningful Life

Solitude	Trustworthy	<u>add your own values</u>
Sophistication	Truth	
Soundness	Truth-seeking	
Speed	Understanding	
Spirit	Unflappability	
Spirit of adventure	Uniqueness	
Spirituality	Unity	
Spontaneity	Usefulness	
Spontaneous	Utility	
Spunk	Valor	
Stability	Variety	
Status	Victory	
Stealth	Vigor	
Stewardship	Virtue	
Stillness	Vision	
Strategic	Vitality	
Strength	Vivacity	
Structure	Volunteering	
Success	Warmheartedness	
Support	Watchfulness	
Supremacy	Wealth	
Surprise	Welcoming	
Sustainability	Willfulness	
Sympathy	Willingness	
Synergy	Winning	
Talent	Wisdom	
Teaching	Wittiness	
Teamwork	Wonder	
Temperance	Worthiness	
Thankful	Youthfulness	
Thankfulness	Zeal	
Thorough		
Thoroughness		
Thoughtful		
Thoughtfulness		
Thrift		
Tidiness		
Timeliness		
Tolerance		
Toughness		
Traditional		
Traditionalism		
Tranquility		
Transcendence		
Transparency		
Trust		
Trustworthiness		

now start listing a few of your

RELATIONSHIPS

PLACES

EVENTS

BELIEFS

MOTIVATIONS

PRACTICES

(add to or refer to your lists anytime)

THIS IS WHAT _________________ MEANS TO ME:

THAT IS WHAT _______________ MEANS TO ME.

THIS IS WHAT _________________ MEANS TO ME:

THAT IS WHAT _______________ MEANS TO ME.

THIS IS WHAT _____________________ MEANS TO ME:

THAT IS WHAT _____________________ MEANS TO ME.

THIS IS WHAT _________________ MEANS TO ME:

THAT IS WHAT _________________ MEANS TO ME.

THIS IS WHAT _______________ MEANS TO ME:

THAT IS WHAT _______________ MEANS TO ME.

THIS IS WHAT _________________ MEANS TO ME:

THAT IS WHAT _______________ MEANS TO ME.

THIS IS WHAT ______________________ MEANS TO ME:

THAT IS WHAT ______________ MEANS TO ME.

THIS IS WHAT _______________________ MEANS TO ME:

THAT IS WHAT _______________________ MEANS TO ME.

THIS IS WHAT _________________ MEANS TO ME:

THAT IS WHAT ________________ MEANS TO ME.

THIS IS WHAT ___________________ MEANS TO ME:

THAT IS WHAT _______________ MEANS TO ME.

THIS IS WHAT ________________________ MEANS TO ME:

THAT IS WHAT ________________________ MEANS TO ME.

THIS IS WHAT _________________ MEANS TO ME:

THAT IS WHAT _______________ MEANS TO ME.

THIS IS WHAT _________________ MEANS TO ME:

THAT IS WHAT _________________ MEANS TO ME.

THIS IS WHAT _______________ MEANS TO ME:

THAT IS WHAT _______________ MEANS TO ME.

THIS IS WHAT ________________ MEANS TO ME:

THAT IS WHAT ________________ MEANS TO ME.

THIS IS WHAT _________________ MEANS TO ME:

THAT IS WHAT _________________ MEANS TO ME.

THIS IS WHAT ___________________ MEANS TO ME:

THAT IS WHAT _________________ MEANS TO ME.

THIS IS WHAT _________________ MEANS TO ME:

THAT IS WHAT _________________ MEANS TO ME.

THIS IS WHAT _______________________ MEANS TO ME:

THAT IS WHAT _______________________ MEANS TO ME.

THIS IS WHAT __________________ MEANS TO ME:

THAT IS WHAT ________________ MEANS TO ME.

THIS IS WHAT _________________ MEANS TO ME:

THAT IS WHAT _________________ MEANS TO ME.

THIS IS WHAT _________________ MEANS TO ME:

THAT IS WHAT _________________ MEANS TO ME.

THIS IS WHAT _________________________ MEANS TO ME:

THAT IS WHAT _________________ MEANS TO ME.

THIS IS WHAT ________________ MEANS TO ME:

THAT IS WHAT ________________ MEANS TO ME.

THIS IS WHAT _________________________ MEANS TO ME:

THAT IS WHAT _________________________ MEANS TO ME.

THIS IS WHAT _________________ MEANS TO ME:

THAT IS WHAT _______________ MEANS TO ME.

THIS IS WHAT _________________ MEANS TO ME:

THAT IS WHAT _________________ MEANS TO ME.

THIS IS WHAT ________________ MEANS TO ME:

THAT IS WHAT ________________ MEANS TO ME.

THIS IS WHAT ________________________ MEANS TO ME:

THAT IS WHAT ________________________ MEANS TO ME.

THIS IS WHAT ___________________ MEANS TO ME:

THAT IS WHAT ________________ MEANS TO ME.

THIS IS WHAT _________________ MEANS TO ME:

THAT IS WHAT _______________ MEANS TO ME.

THIS IS WHAT ___________________ MEANS TO ME:

THAT IS WHAT ________________ MEANS TO ME.

THIS IS WHAT _____________________ MEANS TO ME:

THAT IS WHAT _____________________ MEANS TO ME.

THIS IS WHAT ________________________ MEANS TO ME:

THAT IS WHAT ________________________ MEANS TO ME.

THIS IS WHAT _________________ MEANS TO ME:

THAT IS WHAT _______________ MEANS TO ME.

THIS IS WHAT ________________ MEANS TO ME:

THAT IS WHAT ________________ MEANS TO ME.

THIS IS WHAT ________________________ MEANS TO ME:

THAT IS WHAT ____________________ MEANS TO ME.

THIS IS WHAT _________________ MEANS TO ME:

THAT IS WHAT _______________ MEANS TO ME.

THIS IS WHAT _________________ MEANS TO ME:

THAT IS WHAT _______________ MEANS TO ME.

THIS IS WHAT _________________ MEANS TO ME:

THAT IS WHAT _______________ MEANS TO ME.

THIS IS WHAT ___________________ MEANS TO ME:

THAT IS WHAT ___________________ MEANS TO ME.

THIS IS WHAT _________________ MEANS TO ME:

THAT IS WHAT _______________ MEANS TO ME.

THIS IS WHAT ___________________ MEANS TO ME:

THAT IS WHAT ___________________ MEANS TO ME.

THIS IS WHAT _________________ MEANS TO ME:

THAT IS WHAT _________________ MEANS TO ME.

THIS IS WHAT _____________________ MEANS TO ME:

THAT IS WHAT _________________ MEANS TO ME.

THIS IS WHAT _____________________ MEANS TO ME:

THAT IS WHAT _________________ MEANS TO ME.

THIS IS WHAT ________________ MEANS TO ME:

THAT IS WHAT ________________ MEANS TO ME.

THIS IS WHAT _________________ MEANS TO ME:

THAT IS WHAT _______________ MEANS TO ME.

THIS IS WHAT _________________ MEANS TO ME:

THAT IS WHAT _________________ MEANS TO ME.

THIS IS WHAT ___________________ MEANS TO ME:

THAT IS WHAT _________________ MEANS TO ME.

THIS IS WHAT _______________ MEANS TO ME:

THAT IS WHAT _______________ MEANS TO ME.

THIS IS WHAT _________________ MEANS TO ME:

THAT IS WHAT ________________ MEANS TO ME.

THIS IS WHAT ________________ MEANS TO ME:

THAT IS WHAT ________________ MEANS TO ME.

THIS IS WHAT ___________________ MEANS TO ME:

THAT IS WHAT _________________ MEANS TO ME.

THIS IS WHAT _____________________ MEANS TO ME:

THAT IS WHAT _____________________ MEANS TO ME.

THIS IS WHAT _________________ MEANS TO ME:

THAT IS WHAT _________________ MEANS TO ME.

THIS IS WHAT ________________ MEANS TO ME:

THAT IS WHAT ________________ MEANS TO ME.

THIS IS WHAT _____________________ MEANS TO ME:

THAT IS WHAT _____________________ MEANS TO ME.

THIS IS WHAT ________________ MEANS TO ME:

THAT IS WHAT ________________ MEANS TO ME.

THIS IS WHAT _________________ MEANS TO ME:

THAT IS WHAT _______________ MEANS TO ME.

THIS IS WHAT ________________ MEANS TO ME:

THAT IS WHAT ______________ MEANS TO ME.

THIS IS WHAT _____________________ MEANS TO ME:

THAT IS WHAT _________________ MEANS TO ME.

THIS IS WHAT _________________ MEANS TO ME:

THAT IS WHAT _______________ MEANS TO ME.

THIS IS WHAT _________________ MEANS TO ME:

THAT IS WHAT _______________ MEANS TO ME.

THIS IS WHAT ___________________ MEANS TO ME:

THAT IS WHAT _________________ MEANS TO ME.

THIS IS WHAT _________________ MEANS TO ME:

THAT IS WHAT _________________ MEANS TO ME.

THIS IS WHAT _________________ MEANS TO ME:

THAT IS WHAT _______________ MEANS TO ME.

THIS IS WHAT _____________________ MEANS TO ME:

THAT IS WHAT _____________________ MEANS TO ME.

THIS IS WHAT _____________________ MEANS TO ME:

THAT IS WHAT _____________________ MEANS TO ME.

THIS IS WHAT ________________ MEANS TO ME:

THAT IS WHAT ________________ MEANS TO ME.

THIS IS WHAT _________________ MEANS TO ME:

THAT IS WHAT _________________ MEANS TO ME.

THIS IS WHAT _________________ MEANS TO ME:

THAT IS WHAT _______________ MEANS TO ME.

THIS IS WHAT ________________________ MEANS TO ME:

THAT IS WHAT ________________________ MEANS TO ME.

THIS IS WHAT _________________ MEANS TO ME:

THAT IS WHAT _________________ MEANS TO ME.

THIS IS WHAT _______________________ MEANS TO ME:

THAT IS WHAT _______________________ MEANS TO ME.

THIS IS WHAT _________________ MEANS TO ME:

THAT IS WHAT _________________ MEANS TO ME.

THIS IS WHAT ________________ MEANS TO ME:

THAT IS WHAT ________________ MEANS TO ME.

THIS IS WHAT _________________ MEANS TO ME:

THAT IS WHAT _________________ MEANS TO ME.

THIS IS WHAT _________________ MEANS TO ME:

THAT IS WHAT _______________ MEANS TO ME.

THIS IS WHAT _________________ MEANS TO ME:

THAT IS WHAT _________________ MEANS TO ME.

THIS IS WHAT _________________ MEANS TO ME:

THAT IS WHAT _________________ MEANS TO ME.

THIS IS WHAT _________________ MEANS TO ME:

THAT IS WHAT _________________ MEANS TO ME.

THIS IS WHAT _________________________ MEANS TO ME:

THAT IS WHAT _________________________ MEANS TO ME.

THIS IS WHAT ____________________ MEANS TO ME:

THAT IS WHAT ________________ MEANS TO ME.

THIS IS WHAT _________________ MEANS TO ME:

THAT IS WHAT _________________ MEANS TO ME.

THIS IS WHAT _________________ MEANS TO ME:

THAT IS WHAT _________________ MEANS TO ME.

THIS IS WHAT _____________________ MEANS TO ME:

THAT IS WHAT ___________________ MEANS TO ME.

THIS IS WHAT _________________ MEANS TO ME:

THAT IS WHAT _________________ MEANS TO ME.

THIS IS WHAT _________________ MEANS TO ME:

THAT IS WHAT _________________ MEANS TO ME.

THIS IS WHAT _________________ MEANS TO ME:

THAT IS WHAT _________________ MEANS TO ME.

THIS IS WHAT ________________ MEANS TO ME:

THAT IS WHAT ________________ MEANS TO ME.

THIS IS WHAT _________________ MEANS TO ME:

THAT IS WHAT _______________ MEANS TO ME.

THIS IS WHAT ________________________ MEANS TO ME:

THAT IS WHAT ________________________ MEANS TO ME.

THIS IS WHAT _________________ MEANS TO ME:

THAT IS WHAT _______________ MEANS TO ME.

THIS IS WHAT _________________ MEANS TO ME:

THAT IS WHAT _______________ MEANS TO ME.

THIS IS WHAT _____________________ MEANS TO ME:

THAT IS WHAT _________________ MEANS TO ME.

THIS IS WHAT _______________________ MEANS TO ME:

THAT IS WHAT _______________________ MEANS TO ME.

THIS IS WHAT _________________ MEANS TO ME:

THAT IS WHAT _________________ MEANS TO ME.

THIS IS WHAT _________________ MEANS TO ME:

THAT IS WHAT _______________ MEANS TO ME.

THIS IS WHAT _________________ MEANS TO ME:

THAT IS WHAT _______________ MEANS TO ME.

THIS IS WHAT _______________________ MEANS TO ME:

THAT IS WHAT _______________________ MEANS TO ME.

THIS IS WHAT ________________ MEANS TO ME:

THAT IS WHAT ________________ MEANS TO ME.

THIS IS WHAT _________________ MEANS TO ME:

THAT IS WHAT _________________ MEANS TO ME.

THIS IS WHAT ________________________ MEANS TO ME:

THAT IS WHAT ________________ MEANS TO ME.

THIS IS WHAT _________________________ MEANS TO ME:

THAT IS WHAT _________________________ MEANS TO ME.

THIS IS WHAT _________________ MEANS TO ME:

THAT IS WHAT _________________ MEANS TO ME.

THIS IS WHAT _________________ MEANS TO ME:

THAT IS WHAT _______________ MEANS TO ME.

THIS IS WHAT _________________ MEANS TO ME:

THAT IS WHAT _________________ MEANS TO ME.

THIS IS WHAT ________________________ MEANS TO ME:

THAT IS WHAT ________________________ MEANS TO ME.

THIS IS WHAT _________________ MEANS TO ME:

THAT IS WHAT _______________ MEANS TO ME.

THIS IS WHAT ___________________ MEANS TO ME:

THAT IS WHAT ___________________ MEANS TO ME.

THIS IS WHAT _________________ MEANS TO ME:

THAT IS WHAT _______________ MEANS TO ME.

THIS IS WHAT _________________ MEANS TO ME:

THAT IS WHAT _______________ MEANS TO ME.

THIS IS WHAT ___________________ MEANS TO ME:

THAT IS WHAT ________________ MEANS TO ME.

THIS IS WHAT ___________________ MEANS TO ME:

THAT IS WHAT _________________ MEANS TO ME.

THIS IS WHAT ___________________ MEANS TO ME:

THAT IS WHAT _________________ MEANS TO ME.

THIS IS WHAT ___________________ MEANS TO ME:

THAT IS WHAT ___________________ MEANS TO ME.

THIS IS WHAT _________________ MEANS TO ME:

THAT IS WHAT _______________ MEANS TO ME.

THIS IS WHAT ________________ MEANS TO ME:

THAT IS WHAT ________________ MEANS TO ME.

THIS IS WHAT _________________ MEANS TO ME:

THAT IS WHAT _________________ MEANS TO ME.

THIS IS WHAT _________________ MEANS TO ME:

THAT IS WHAT _________________ MEANS TO ME.

THIS IS WHAT __________________ MEANS TO ME:

THAT IS WHAT _________________ MEANS TO ME.

THIS IS WHAT ________________ MEANS TO ME:

THAT IS WHAT ________________ MEANS TO ME.

THIS IS WHAT _________________ MEANS TO ME:

THAT IS WHAT _______________ MEANS TO ME.

THIS IS WHAT _________________ MEANS TO ME:

THAT IS WHAT _______________ MEANS TO ME.

THIS IS WHAT _________________ MEANS TO ME:

THAT IS WHAT _________________ MEANS TO ME.

THIS IS WHAT _________________ MEANS TO ME:

THAT IS WHAT _______________ MEANS TO ME.

THIS IS WHAT _________________ MEANS TO ME:

THAT IS WHAT _________________ MEANS TO ME.

THIS IS WHAT _______________________ MEANS TO ME:

THAT IS WHAT _______________________ MEANS TO ME.

THIS IS WHAT _________________ MEANS TO ME:

THAT IS WHAT _______________ MEANS TO ME.

THIS IS WHAT _____________________ MEANS TO ME:

THAT IS WHAT _________________ MEANS TO ME.

THIS IS WHAT _________________ MEANS TO ME:

THAT IS WHAT _________________ MEANS TO ME.

THIS IS WHAT _________________ MEANS TO ME:

THAT IS WHAT _________________ MEANS TO ME.

THIS IS WHAT ___________________ MEANS TO ME:

THAT IS WHAT ___________________ MEANS TO ME.

THIS IS WHAT ________________________ MEANS TO ME:

THAT IS WHAT ________________________ MEANS TO ME.

THIS IS WHAT ________________ MEANS TO ME:

THAT IS WHAT ________________ MEANS TO ME.

THIS IS WHAT _______________________ MEANS TO ME:

THAT IS WHAT _______________________ MEANS TO ME.

THIS IS WHAT _________________ MEANS TO ME:

THAT IS WHAT _______________ MEANS TO ME.

THIS IS WHAT ________________________ MEANS TO ME:

THAT IS WHAT ________________________ MEANS TO ME.

THIS IS WHAT _________________ MEANS TO ME:

THAT IS WHAT _______________ MEANS TO ME.

THIS IS WHAT _________________________ MEANS TO ME:

THAT IS WHAT _________________________ MEANS TO ME.

THIS IS WHAT ___________________ MEANS TO ME:

THAT IS WHAT _________________ MEANS TO ME.

THIS IS WHAT _________________ MEANS TO ME:

THAT IS WHAT _______________ MEANS TO ME.

THIS IS WHAT ________________ MEANS TO ME:

THAT IS WHAT ________________ MEANS TO ME.

THIS IS WHAT _________________ MEANS TO ME:

THAT IS WHAT ________________ MEANS TO ME.

THIS IS WHAT _________________ MEANS TO ME:

THAT IS WHAT _________________ MEANS TO ME.

THIS IS WHAT ________________________ MEANS TO ME:

THAT IS WHAT ________________________ MEANS TO ME.

THIS IS WHAT _________________ MEANS TO ME:

THAT IS WHAT ________________ MEANS TO ME.

THIS IS WHAT ________________ MEANS TO ME:

THAT IS WHAT ________________ MEANS TO ME.

THIS IS WHAT _________________ MEANS TO ME:

THAT IS WHAT _________________ MEANS TO ME.

www.ingramcontent.com/pod-product-compliance
Lightning Source LLC
Chambersburg PA
CBHW070521160726
48003CB00004B/1652